THE APPARITIONS OF MARY

Nihil Obstat: Reverend Michael L. Diskin, Assistant Chancellor
Imprimatur: Most Reverend Thomas J. Olmsted, Bishop of Phoenix
Date: February 13, 2015

By Bart Tesoriero
Illustrated by Miguel D. Lopez

ISBN 978-1-61796-159-5
© Copyright 2015 by Aquinas Kids, Phoenix, Arizona.
Printed in China

Mary

A long time ago, there lived a lovely young lady in Nazareth. Her name was Mary. She was engaged to a carpenter named Joseph. One day, God sent the angel Gabriel on a very important mission to Mary. Gabriel told Mary that God had chosen her to be the mother of His Son. Mary said, "How can this be? I am a virgin!" The angel replied, "The Holy Spirit will come upon you in power. Your child will be holy." Mary said, "I am the handmaid of the Lord. Let it be done unto me according to your word." With that the angel left her.

Some months later, the Roman ruler, Caesar Augustus, ordered that a census be taken to find out how many people lived in the empire. Everyone had to go to the birthplace of their ancestors to be enrolled.

Joseph and Mary left Nazareth and journeyed to the city of David, called Bethlehem, because Joseph was of the house and family of David. Every inn and house of that little town was full, and they found no place to stay. Mary was very tired. Finally Joseph found a little stable with a manger in it where the animals were fed. He did his best to make it comfortable for Mary, who laid down to rest.

Jesus

That night, Mary gave birth to her son, Jesus. She wrapped Him in warm clothing and laid Him in the manger. In the fields nearby, shepherds were watching their flocks when suddenly the angel of the Lord came to them in a bright light. "Do not be afraid!" the angel said. "Behold, I bring you good news of great joy: Today in the city of David a savior is born for you who is Messiah and Lord."

When Jesus was about 30 years old, He was baptized by John the Baptist. After that, the Holy Spirit led Jesus into the desert to be tested. He returned filled with the Spirit and power. Jesus called some fishermen by the Sea of Galilee. "Come follow me, and I will make you fishers of men." At once they left their nets and followed Jesus. Jesus called other men as well, and from them He chose the twelve apostles.

Jesus healed all who came to Him, and taught them about God His Father. The people listened eagerly to Jesus. However, the rulers of the people were jealous of Him and did not believe Him. They arrested Jesus and had Him put to death. Jesus died on the cross for all of us, to save us from sin. Mary held Jesus in her arms after His death, as she had held Him at His birth. Jesus was buried in a tomb which had been sealed with a huge stone.

New Life!

Very early in the morning on the first day of the week, following His burial, Jesus arose from the dead! After His resurrection, Jesus remained on the earth, speaking to His disciples about the kingdom of God. After 40 days, Jesus blessed His apostles and followers. Then He ascended up into heaven in a cloud to return to His Father.

The apostles returned to Jerusalem. Mother Mary was with them, along with others who believed. When the day of Pentecost came, they were all in one room together. Suddenly a noise like a strong driving wind came from the sky and filled the room. Tongues as of fire appeared, which parted and rested on each one of them. All of them were filled with the Holy Spirit! They began to speak in different tongues, as the Spirit enabled them to proclaim. Peter and the apostles boldly preached about Jesus, the Son of God. The Church was born!

Finally the time came for Mary to leave this earth. When Mary's life was over, God took her, body and soul, into heaven. Jesus crowned Mary as the Queen of all the angels and saints. She is the Queen of heaven and earth. Mary continues to love us as our Mother in heaven. She helps us when we need her and whenever we pray for her aid. She wants to help all of us feel the love of Jesus in our hearts. She wants to help us to love and obey Him.

Our Lady of Mount Carmel

From heaven, Mary has sometimes visited the earth. These visits are called apparitions. Mary appears to help us when we need her and whenever God wants to give us a special message through her.

A long time ago, Saint Simon Stock was the head of the Carmelite Order, a group of priests and brothers dedicated to Mary. One day our Blessed Mother appeared to him, and gave him a brown woolen scapular. A scapular was like a small apron that people would wear over their clothes to keep them clean. Mary said to Saint Simon, "Receive, my beloved son, the Scapular of your Order. It is the special sign of my favor, which I have obtained for you and your children of Mount Carmel. It is a sign of salvation, a sure safeguard in danger, a pledge of peace and my special protection until the end of the ages."

The Church decided that anyone who wanted to could wear a smaller Scapular, and receive the Scapular promise. The Scapular is a sign that we want to consecrate our hearts to Mary. Often children will be given a Brown Scapular on their First Communion Day.

Our Lady of Guadalupe

Juan Diego was a poor Aztec Indian born in 1474. Franciscan priests from Spain preached to the Aztecs about Jesus and the Catholic Faith. Juan Diego, his wife, and his uncle believed the Gospel. They accepted Jesus as their Savior and were baptized in 1525. Sadly, Juan's wife died, and Juan went to live near his uncle, who had become very sick. Juan had a deep love for Jesus in the Eucharist and walked miles to attend Mass, even on weekdays.

On Saturday morning, December 9th, 1531, Juan left for Mass as usual. As he ran up a small hill called Tepeyac, some say that Juan heard the sweet shrill song of birds chirping at the first light of dawn. Suddenly their song ended. From the top of the hill, Juan heard the voice of a young woman calling his name: "Juanito!"

Juan climbed to the top of the hill. As he looked up, he saw rays like the sun beaming brightly around the head and feet of a young Indian girl. She was about 16 years old and so very beautiful! She wore a blue cape covered in stars. She appeared to be an Aztec princess. The beautiful Lady said, "Juan, smallest and dearest of my little children, where are you going? Dear little son, I love you. I am the ever-Virgin Mary, Mother of the true God who gives life."

The Lady continued, "God made everything and He is in all places. He is the Lord of heaven and earth. I desire a temple, a church, in this place where I will show my love to your people. I want to show my compassion to all people who ask my help. Here I will see their tears. I will console them and they will be at ease. Run now to tell the bishop all you have seen and heard." Juan Diego ran as fast as he could to the palace of Bishop Zumarraga.

The bishop listened kindly to Juan, and said he would think about his request. Juan returned home, sad that the bishop did not believe him. The beautiful Lady appeared to Juan, and told him to ask the bishop again.

This time, the bishop said, "Ask the Lady for a sign." Juan knelt before Our Lady and told her of the bishop's request. She said, "Very well, my little son. Come back tomorrow and I will give you a sign."

Juan feared that his uncle was dying, and did not return the next morning. Early Tuesday morning, December 12th, as Juan Diego ran past the hill of Tepeyac, the Blessed Mother appeared to him again. "My little son," she said, "do not be afraid. Am I not here who am your Mother? Are you not under my protection? Your uncle will not die. At this very moment he is cured."

Mary told Juan to climb the hill and cut the flowers growing there. Juan knew that no flowers ever grew in the cold winter, but there, before him, were beautiful roses! Juan cut them and put them in his cloak, called a tilma. Mary arranged the roses tenderly with her own hands, and told Juan to bring them to the bishop.

Juan Diego untied his tilma and the roses tumbled out before the bishop. Bishop Zumarraga fell to his knees, as did his servants. They pointed to Juan's cloak in awe. Juan looked down in front of him. To his surprise he saw the Virgin herself, imprinted on his tilma!

The Bishop built a church to honor our Lady. Many people came to see the miracle and to pray before the image of the beautiful Lady. Juan Diego told his fellow Aztecs and the other Indians the story of Our Lady of Guadalupe. He urged them to accept Jesus and the Catholic Faith. Juan explained that Mary was the Mother of the true God. The natives learned that God had sent his only Son to die for all people. His one sacrifice saved them all.

Many of the Indians believed and were baptized, sometimes thousands of them in a single day! Within 50 years, eight million Indians converted, and Our Lady of Guadalupe took her place in the souls of her children.

Our Lady of Lourdes

Bernadette Marie Soubirous was born on January 7, 1844, to a poor family in Lourdes, a small village in France. She was a quiet, modest girl with a good sense of humor.

On the 11th of February, 1858, Bernadette went with her sister Marie and a friend to gather firewood on the banks of the river that flowed near her home. The two girls went ahead and Bernadette found herself alone, across from a grotto of rock rising from the earth. Suddenly, Bernadette heard the sound of a rushing wind and saw a golden cloud moving out from the cave behind the grotto. To her amazement, Bernadette saw a beautiful Lady clothed in a blue and white dress appear above a rose bush. The Lady smiled at Bernadette and made the Sign of the Cross with a golden rosary. Bernadette knelt down and began to pray. The Lady fingered her rosary with Bernadette and smiled.

The Lady asked Bernadette to come to the grotto for 15 days. She told Bernadette, "I promise you happiness, not in this world but in the next." She continued, "I would like to see many people come here." In her sixth appearance, the Lady said, "Pray much for poor sinners," which Bernadette did from then on.

On February 25th, 1844, the Lady told Bernadette, "Drink from the fountain and bathe in it." Bernadette scratched in the loose gravel and soon a little pool of water formed, with bubbles rising from it. Bernadette drank from the water and washed her face. In two days the pool became a stream. Within two weeks a blind man was healed. Soon after that, a dying child was restored to health!

The Lady asked Bernadette to have a chapel built on the site of the grotto. She said that people should walk there in procession. Bernadette told this to her pastor, who directed Bernadette to ask the Lady her name. The Lady said, "I am the Immaculate Conception." She was the Virgin Mary!

Bernadette repeated the Lady's name to the priest, who responded, "Can you ever forgive me for doubting your visions of the Mother of God?" Bernadette saw Our Lady two more times. Bernadette joined the Sisters of Charity and died there in the convent at the young age of 35.

Each year more than five million pilgrims travel to Lourdes. They honor our Mother Mary and ask her help as they seek healing of spirit, soul, and body. The water from the spring continues to show remarkable healing power to this day, bringing healings to many people. Pope Pius XI canonized Saint Bernadette in 1933.

Our Lady of Fatima

On May 13th, 1917, the Blessed Virgin Mary appeared to three little shepherds in the village of Fatima, Portugal. Seven-year old Jacinta, her nine-year-old brother Francisco, and their ten-year-old cousin Lucia were tending their sheep in a field called the Cova da Iria. Suddenly they saw a bright flash of light. A beautiful Lady, dressed in white and gold, appeared on a cloud over a small oak tree! A golden cord hung around her neck. Her hands were joined in prayer and she held a pearl rosary.

The Lady smiled at the children and said, "Have no fear, I will do you no harm. I come from heaven, and I would like you to come here on the 13th of each month, until October. Then I will tell you who I am."

The news spread, and the next month, about 70 people accompanied the children. This time, the beautiful Lady from heaven asked the children to pray the Rosary often. She taught them a special prayer to pray after each decade. We now call it the Fatima Prayer.

The Fatima Prayer

O my Jesus, forgive us our sins; save us from the fires of hell. Lead all souls to Heaven, especially those most in need of Your mercy.

The Lady urged the children to pray the Rosary for the ending of World War I. She also promised that she would work a great miracle at the Cova in October, the month of the Holy Rosary. Our Lady said that the Lord wanted people to be devoted to her Immaculate Heart. Mary asked people to attend Mass and receive Holy Communion on the first Saturday of each month. She promised that Russia would be converted if people obeyed her requests, and there would be peace.

On August 13th, more than 15,000 people gathered at the Cova da Iria. The mayor of Fatima, who was against the Church, had kidnapped Lucia, Francisco, and Jacinta, and had them put into prison. However, in a few days they were released and Mother Mary appeared to them. She requested that a new church be built in her honor.

On September 13th, more than 30,000 people gathered at the Cova da Iria. Once more the Blessed Virgin came from heaven and told the children to pray the Rosary for the ending of the war.

A heavy rain fell all night and into the morning as a great crowd of more than 70,000 people gathered at the Cova on October 13th, 1917. The Lady appeared to the children for the last time, more radiant than ever. "Her face was brighter than the sun," said Francisco.

"I am the Lady of the Rosary," the Virgin Mary said. "I have come to warn the faithful to amend their lives and ask pardon for their sins. They must not continue to offend Our Lord, who has been so deeply offended. They must pray the rosary." She repeated that she wished a church to be built at Fatima in her honor. She said that if people amended their lives, the war would end soon. She then left the children, raising her hands toward the sky.

Someone cried, "Look at the sun!" The children looked up and saw Mother Mary with Saint Joseph and the Infant Jesus. They saw Jesus blessing the people.

Meanwhile, the people were able to look at the sun without hurting their eyes. It appeared as a silver disc, and began spinning in the sky. As it danced, it cast off great shafts of colored light which flashed and fell upon the sky and the earth. Men and women fell to their knees and prayed as brilliant colors fell on the trees and stones. Suddenly, the sun began to zigzag! It started to fall like a wheel of fire upon the people. They cried out in fear and asked Jesus and Mary to save them. After a few moments, the sun returned to its place. The people rejoiced and praised God for the "Miracle of the Sun."

Today people come from all over the world to pray at the basilica of Fatima, and to honor Our Lady of the Rosary.

The Rosary

Over the centuries, Mother Mary has appeared many times, always asking us to pray. When we pray to Mary, she leads us to Jesus her Son. It is good for us to pray every day to Mary. We do not worship her, but we do ask her to help us to love and serve God more. When we feel afraid, she helps us to feel strong. When we feel sad, she helps us to feel joy. When we feel selfish, she helps us to serve others. She wants to help us get to heaven, to live forever with God and all His holy ones.

The Rosary is a very special prayer! When we pray the Rosary, we think about events in the lives of Jesus and Mary. We call these events "mysteries," because they teach us something about the love of God. As we pray, we open up our hearts to Jesus and Mary, and we let them teach us.

A long time ago, monks prayed the 150 Psalms as part of their daily prayer. Catholics who worked and had families wanted to pray too, so they replaced the Psalms with the Our Father, the Hail Mary, and the Gloria. They kept count using a Rosary, which is a string of beads from which hangs a crucifix.

As you pray the Rosary, it is good to think about each of the mysteries. You will see how much God loves you and how special Mother Mary is, who leads you to her Son!

How to Pray the Rosary

- Make the Sign of the Cross and pray the Apostles' Creed, while holding the crucifix.
- Pray one Our Father on the first bead, three Hail Marys on the next three beads for the virtues of Faith, Hope, and Charity, and finish with a Glory Be.
- Announce the first Mystery. Pause for a moment to think about it. Then pray an Our Father on the large bead, ten Hail Marys on the smaller beads, and finish with a Glory Be. This is one decade.
- If you wish, pray the Fatima Prayer, found on page 21, after the Glory Be.
- Continue in this way until all you have prayed all five decades. To finish, pray the Hail Holy Queen, found on page 32.

There are 20 Mysteries of the Rosary. We usually pray the **Joyful Mysteries** of the Rosary on Mondays and Saturdays. We pray the **Luminous Mysteries** on Thursdays. We pray the **Sorrowful Mysteries** on Tuesdays and Fridays. We pray the **Glorious Mysteries** on Wednesdays and Sundays.

The Joyful Mysteries

The Annunciation
The Visitation
The Birth of Jesus
The Presentation of Jesus
The Finding of Jesus in the Temple

The Luminous Mysteries

The Baptism of Jesus
The Wedding at Cana
The Proclamation of the Kingdom
The Transfiguration
The Institution of the Eucharist

The Sorrowful Mysteries

The Agony in the Garden
The Scourging at the Pillar
The Crowning with Thorns
The Carrying of the Cross
The Crucifixion

The Glorious Mysteries

The Resurrection of Jesus
The Ascension of Jesus
The Descent of the Holy Spirit
The Assumption of Mary
The Coronation of Mary

Hail, Holy Queen

Hail, Holy Queen, Mother of Mercy,

Our life, our sweetness, and our hope!

To thee do we cry,

poor banished children of Eve;

to thee do we send up our sighs,

mourning and weeping in this valley of tears.

Turn then, most gracious advocate,

thine eyes of mercy towards us;

and after this our exile, show unto us

the blessed fruit of thy womb, Jesus;

O clement, O loving, O sweet Virgin Mary.